I0815804

JÉRÔME LEJEUNE

THE SAINTLY GENETICIST

Published by Word on Fire Votive, an imprint of
Word on Fire, Elk Grove Village, IL 60007

Printed in italy

Cover design, typesetting, and interior art direction by Nicolas Fredrickson and Rozann Lee
Editing by Haley Stewart

First published June 2024
Reprinted June 2024

ISBN: 978-1-68578-097-5

Library of Congress Control Number: 2023945291

ANA BRAGA-HENEBRY ILLUSTRATIONS BY ANITA BARGHIGIANI

JÉRÔME LEJEUNE

THE SAINTLY GENETICIST

Author's Note

At a conference in 1993, my husband and I personally met Dr. Jérôme Lejeune, who was a keynote speaker. The conversation with him at the table was polite and fascinating, and his blue, smiling eyes radiated joy. We never forgot that encounter. What a delight now to bring his life story to young readers!

Dedication

This book is dedicated to my grandson James and to children with Down syndrome and other medically complex conditions. May they have the good fortune of finding health professionals as caring as Venerable Dr. Lejeune.

Jérôme Lejeune loved to learn, but when war broke out in France in 1940, he couldn't go to school. His father decided to teach Jérôme and his brothers, Philippe and Remy, at home.

The boys read the old classics and learned languages. They had music, astronomy, and mathematics lessons. Everything fascinated Jérôme! He started to dream of studying medicine and one day becoming a doctor.

Jérôme studied very hard when he got to medical school. He loved the calm quiet of the library in Paris. One day when he stopped by in search of a book, he found something else: a young woman named Birthe.

Birthe's joy and goodness enchanted Jérôme, and soon they fell in love. After many months, they were married. The Lejeunes were blessed with five children.

After many years of work and study, Jérôme became a pediatrician, a doctor who cares for children. He started seeing young patients who had Down syndrome. The children loved Dr. Lejeune because he always treated them with kindness and respect.

Dr. Lejeune was unhappy that so little was known about children with Down syndrome. He saw patients in the morning and worked on his research in the afternoon so he could learn more about this condition.

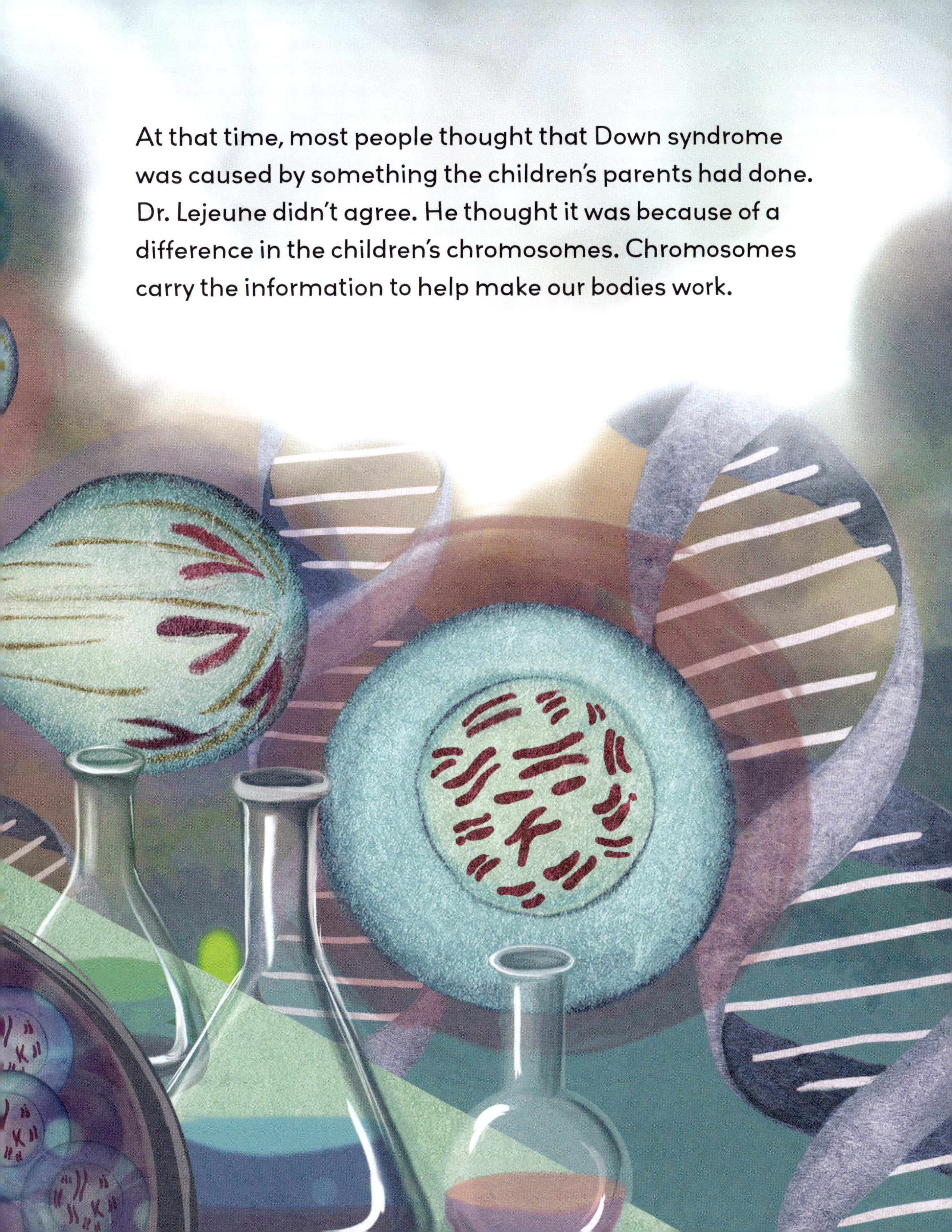

At that time, most people thought that Down syndrome was caused by something the children's parents had done. Dr. Lejeune didn't agree. He thought it was because of a difference in the children's chromosomes. Chromosomes carry the information to help make our bodies work.

I
II
III
IV
V
VI
VII
VIII
IX
X
XI
XII
XIII
XV
XVI
XVIII
XIX
XXI

In order to discover everything he could to help his patients, Dr. Lejeune worked hard in the lab of his boss, Professor Turpin. As he continued his research, Dr. Lejeune learned how to collect the chromosomes from a patient's cells.

Chromosomes are all jumbled up inside our cells, like short pieces of spaghetti. Dr. Lejeune used a new technique, brought to France by his colleague Dr. Marthe Gautier. Using this new method, Dr. Lejeune spread out the chromosomes and colored them. Then he used scissors and glue to cut out the chromosomes. Finally, he arranged and counted them. That is when he made his amazing discovery!

What Dr. Lejeune discovered changed the way we understand Down syndrome and all genetic conditions. Typically, humans have 46 chromosomes matched in 23 pairs. Dr. Lejeune discovered that

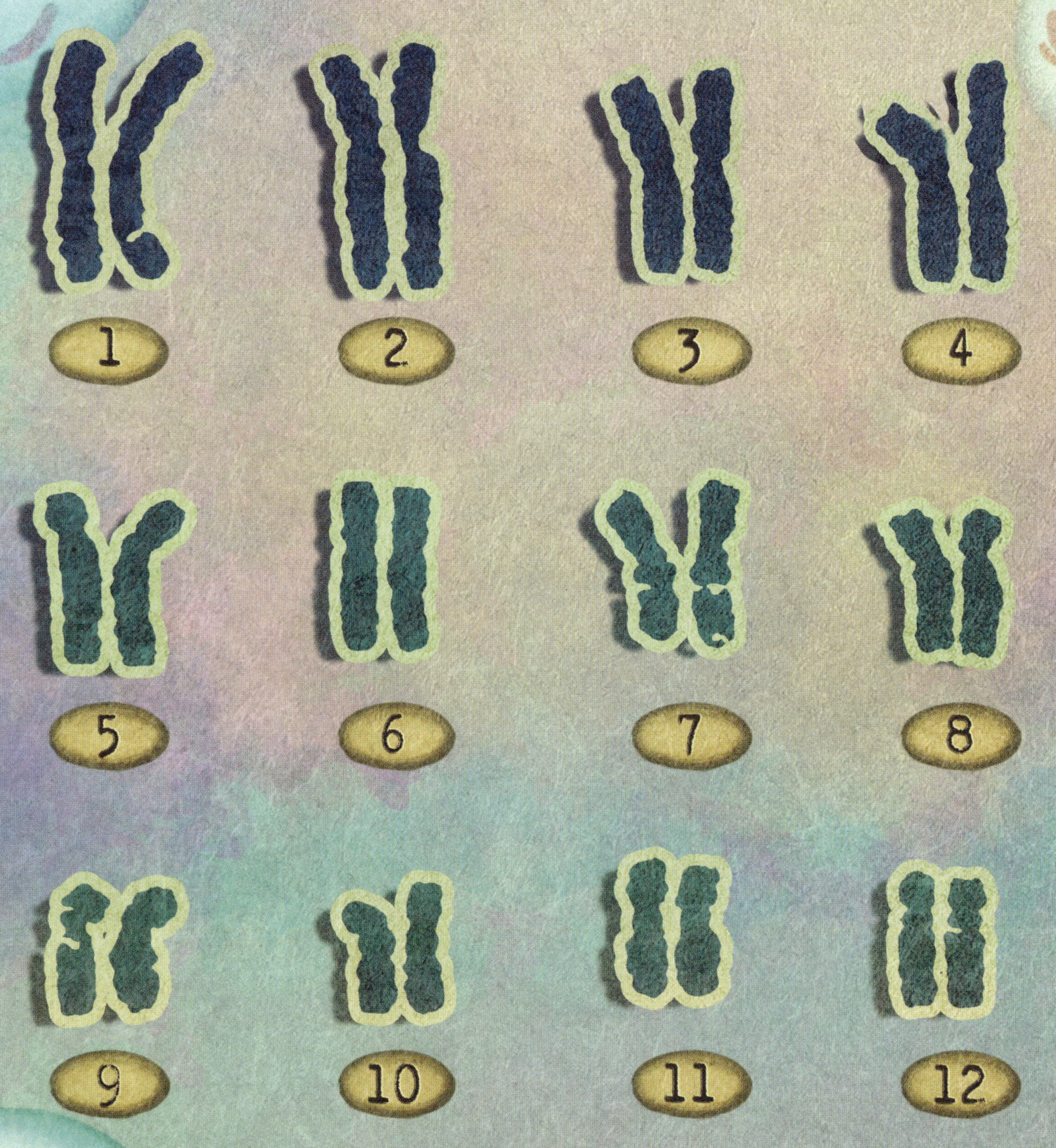

a child with Down syndrome has an extra copy of chromosome 21, the smallest pair of chromosomes. In 1958 Dr. Lejeune proved that there is a genetic cause for Down syndrome, a condition that can sometimes be called Trisomy (three chromosomes) 21.

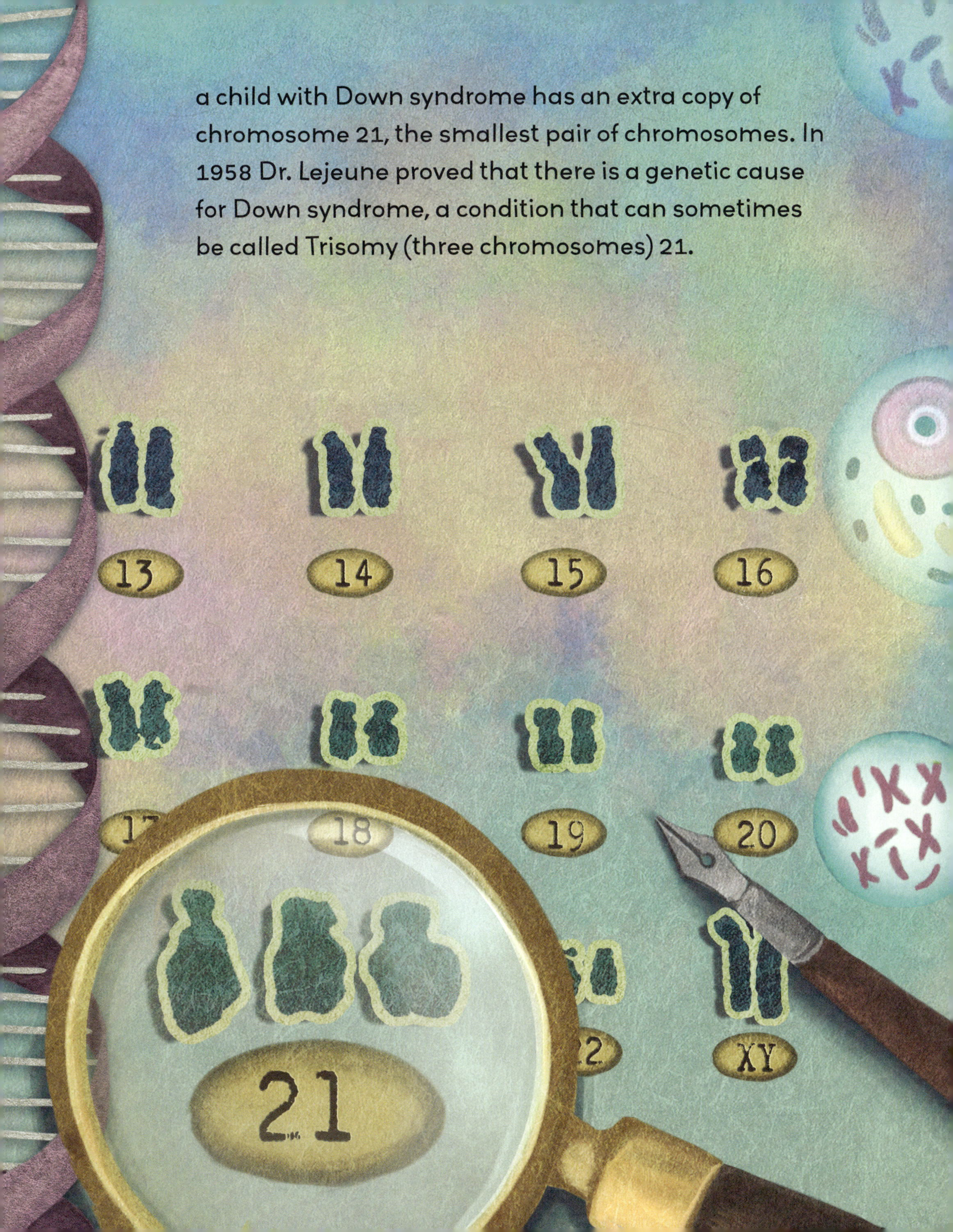

The news of this discovery spread like wildfire around the world. Scientists were very impressed! Some people called Dr. Lejeune the

"father of modern genetics."

He won many prizes. Dr. Lejeune had great plans for using the money from these awards to help his patients and share his work. He believed it was important for everyone to understand that a child is not born with Down syndrome because her parents made a mistake or did anything wrong. He loved his patients and didn't want anyone to be embarrassed or ashamed of this condition.

Even though Dr. Lejeune and Birthe received many invitations to fancy places, their favorite nights were spent with their children at homemade family dinners. Many friends and young medical students were eager to visit the Lejeunes, so Birthe was always pulling up one more chair to the table.

When people began testing babies for chromosomal differences before they were born and making decisions about their future, it made Dr. Lejeune very sad. He knew many would choose to end the lives of babies with Down syndrome before birth. He thought of all his wonderful patients and the joy they brought to everyone around them.

Dr. Lejeune appeared on TV many times to speak about the value of every human life. Many people did not agree with his position and debated him on camera. Dr. Lejeune was firm in his convictions, but he always spoke with respect and love for his opponents.

Life became more difficult for Dr. Lejeune because of his bold words advocating for the dignity of his patients and every human life. Not everyone wanted to hear this message. Some of the support and funding for his research was revoked, but no one could take away his joy and hope.

Dr. Lejeune was Catholic and attended Mass with his family. He would always tell his friends and family that the best way to live was with prayer and faith in God.

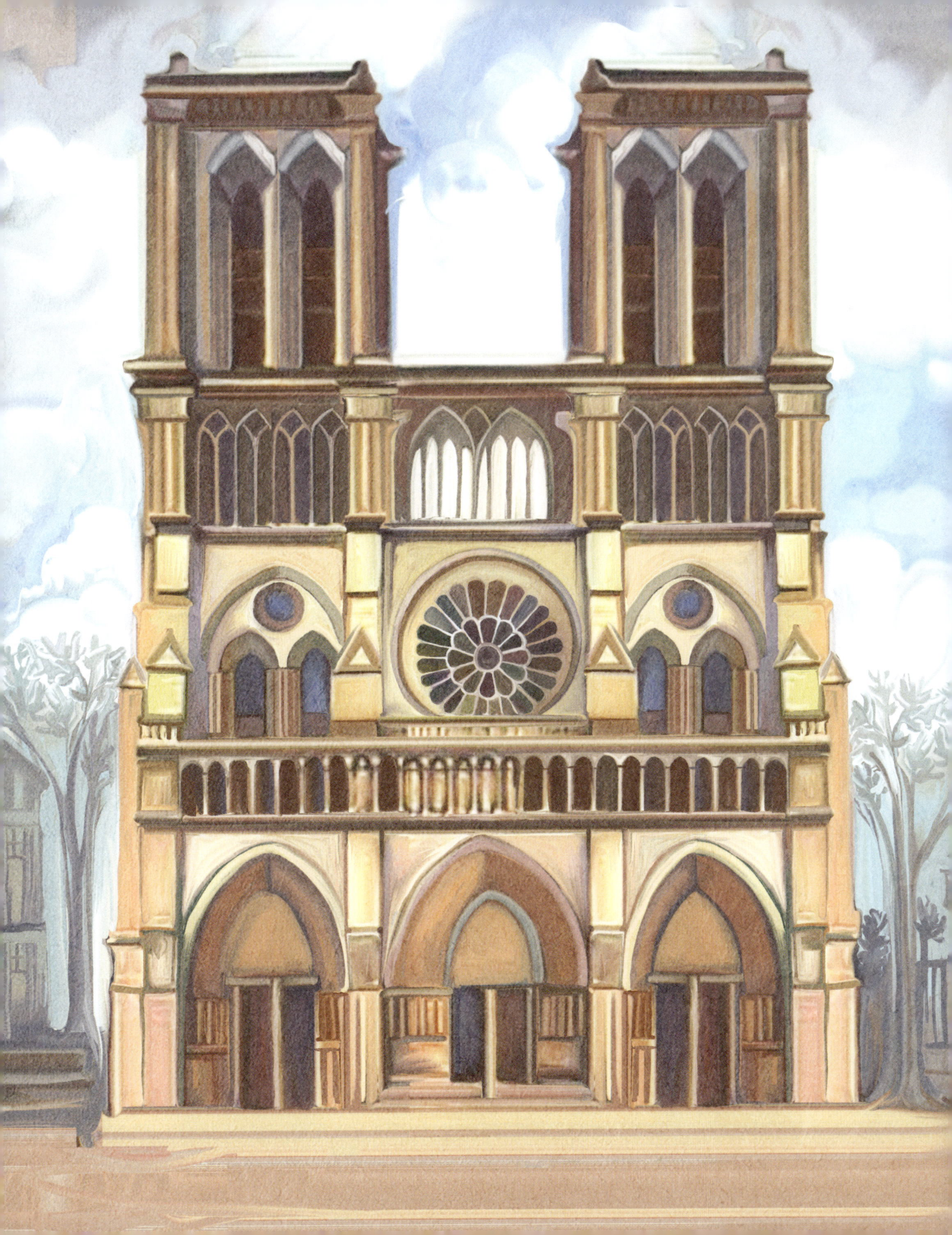

Dr. Lejeune was invited to be a member of the Pontifical Academy of Sciences and met Pope John Paul II. They became close friends right away and shared a great love for God's creation and for the gift of human life. The pope trusted Dr. Lejeune's scientific opinion on many issues.

Another friend was Mother Teresa of Kolkata, the most famous religious sister in the world.

Even with such important friends, Dr. Lejeune chose every day to live a humble and simple life serving his family and his beloved patients.

Dr. Jérôme Lejeune died when he was sixty-seven years old, surrounded by family and friends. Famous people came and spoke at his funeral in the huge and splendid church of Notre Dame in Paris. Many families also came, bringing the children Dr. Lejeune had cared for. During the solemn event, a young man with Trisomy 21 suddenly exclaimed aloud for all to hear:

"Thank you, Dr. Lejeune!
Because of you, I am proud of myself!"

After Dr. Lejeune's death, his wife and children founded the Jérôme Lejeune Foundation and the Jérôme Lejeune Medical Institute. The institute helps thousands of families every year from all over the world. Birthe Lejeune continued her husband's important mission of telling people about the value of every human life.

In 2021 the Catholic Church declared Jérôme Lejeune "**Venerable**," a step closer to being called a saint. Because of this good doctor, we not only know more about genetics, we know what it looks like to live faithfully and bravely in service of life.

TIMELINE OF IMPORTANT EVENTS

1952

Jérôme marries
Birthe Bringsted.

1926

Jérôme Lejeune is born
near Paris, France.

1952

After finishing his
studies in medicine,
Dr. Lejeune becomes
a researcher.

1994

Pope John Paul II names Jérôme
Lejeune the first President of the
Pontifical Academy for Life.

1974

Pope Paul VI names Jérôme
Lejeune a member of the
Pontifical Academy of Sciences.

1994

Jérôme Lejeune dies
on Easter morning.

1958

Dr. Lejeune discovers that people with Trisomy 21 carry an extra chromosome, showing that this condition is genetic.

1964

Dr. Lejeune becomes the first Chair of the Department of Fundamental Genetics at the University of Paris.

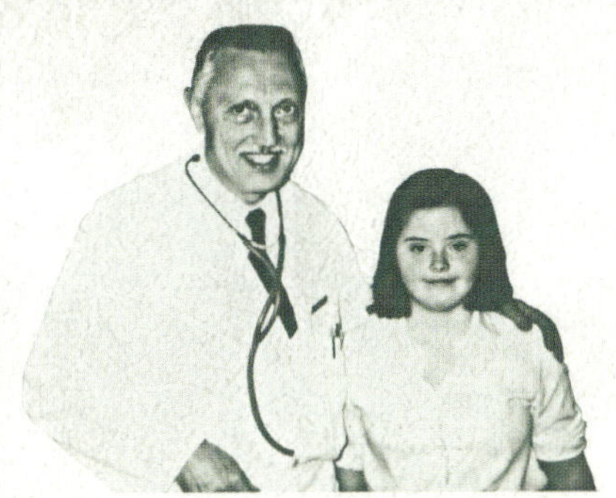

1962

President John F. Kennedy awards the Kennedy Prize personally to Dr. Lejeune.

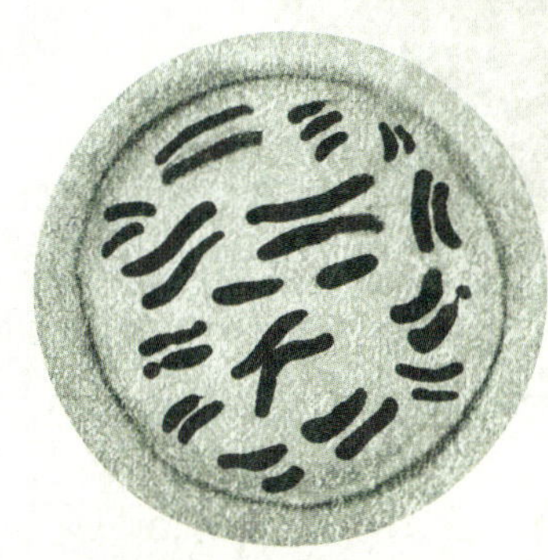

1997

Pope John Paul II, during World Youth Day in France, goes to pray at Jérôme Lejeune's grave near Paris.

2021

Dr. Jérôme Lejeune is declared Venerable by the Catholic Church.

2007

A cause for canonization of Jérôme Lejeune is opened by the Catholic Church.

Afterword
by Mark Bradford

Dear reader, I hope you enjoyed this wonderful story of Dr. Jérôme Lejeune. He is one of my heroes. He wasn't only very smart and wise; he also had a deep love for his patients, for his wife and children, and especially for God.

The Roman Catholic Church has looked very carefully into Dr. Lejeune's life and determined that he was a man of "heroic virtue." Heroic virtue means his soul was courageous and he did what was right—even when it was unpopular and difficult. That's why the Church has given him the title "Venerable," which means that his commitment to following Jesus makes him worthy of honor. In everything he did, he was guided by his deep faith and his obedience in loving people the way God calls us to love.

From this story of his life, you can see that Dr. Lejeune was a brilliant man, but he was also humble. Being admired was not his greatest desire. What was important to him was that the needs of people like his patients would be remembered and that they would be treated with care.

As you have learned, Dr. Lejeune's patients were people with Down syndrome and other disabilities. People with Down syndrome have a little something extra in their chromosomes. Chromosomes are very tiny little things in all our cells that help make us who we are. They determine the color of our eyes, whether our hair is blond or black, how tall we are, and our mental and physical capabilities.

While most of us have forty-six chromosomes, or twenty-three pairs, most people with Down syndrome have forty-seven! From the time they were conceived in their mother's womb, instead of having two chromosomes 21, most have three. The name Down syndrome comes from Dr. John Langdon Down, the man who first described the characteristics of this group of people.

So, what are those characteristics? When you meet someone who has Down syndrome you might be able to tell by the way they look, especially by their faces. I think they have beautiful faces. I have a son with Down syndrome, and he's one of the most handsome young men in the world. And his sense of humor brings so much joy to our family. People with Down syndrome also may be shorter than others, and they learn more slowly than others. Sometimes they can be a little hard to understand when they speak.

Imagine if you were baking a cake that called for two cups of sugar and you put in three instead. It would be a very sweet cake! Chromosomes make something called proteins in our bodies, and proteins are very important. They manage the way our bodies grow and function, and they keep us healthy. They also manage the way our brains work by controlling how our brain cells communicate with one another.

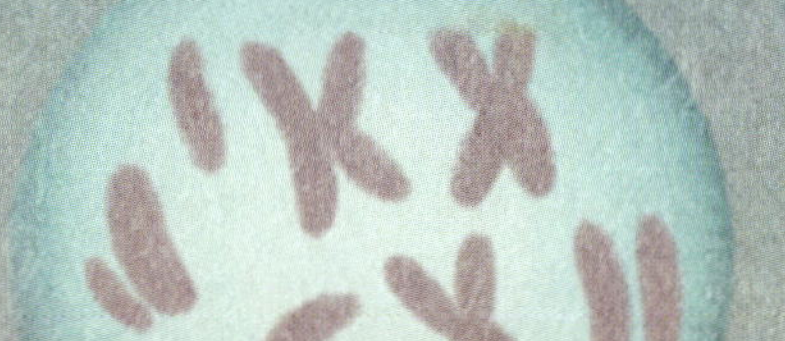

Well, imagine that you have an extra chromosome producing all those extra proteins like a person with Down syndrome has. Like extra sugar in your cake, there are more proteins than the "recipe" calls for. For people with Down syndrome, this results in their unique facial features and sometimes health problems like heart conditions.

We are living in a time when our heroes are people like Dr. Lejeune who are very smart or people who are famous, successful, beautiful, and talented. With his incredible wisdom, Dr. Lejeune would be the first to tell us that those things are not important. God made each of us very special. After all, he made us in his image and sent Jesus to die for us as our Savior. He wants us to love and care for one another no matter how attractive, intelligent, or talented.

People who have Down syndrome are people like you and me who just need a little more love and support. God wants us to love and care for them, just as he loves each of us. Sometimes when we meet people who are different from us, we might feel uncomfortable. But we should never be afraid of people who are different from us because they have a disability like Down syndrome. I can assure you, if you make a friend of someone like my son who has Down syndrome, you will have a wonderful friend for life.

Mark Bradford *is the Fellow for Persons with Intellectual and Developmental Disabilities at the Word on Fire Institute. For over twenty years, he has been blessed to serve in leadership positions in various church ministries, including as the founding president of the Jérôme Lejeune Foundation in the United States. Mark and his wife, Denise, are parents to Thomas, the sixth of seven children (and first son), who happens to have been gifted with an extra 21st chromosome.*

About the Author

ANA BRAGA-HENEBRY grew up the seventh of ten children in Rio de Janeiro and earned an MA in Humanities from The University of Texas at Dallas. Together with her husband Geoff, a scientist and professor, Ana raised seven children. One of their sons is a Marine Corps officer, and one of their daughters a cloistered religious sister. Ana loves to listen to audiobooks while gardening and cooking. A lifelong educator, Ana writes and speaks on various aspects of Catholic culture. She makes their home in East Lansing, Michigan.

About the Illustrator

ANITA BARGHIGIANI graduated from the Florence Academy of Fine Arts. She has illustrated many books, including *Saintly Creatures: 14 Tales of Animals and Their Holy Companions* by Alexi Sargeant. Anita currently lives in the woods between Florence and Bologna, where she works, plays the guitar, and actively helps animals as a volunteer.

Acknowledgments

I must acknowledge many people who helped me with this project. A sincere thanks to the initial input and enthusiasm of my little sister, Sr. Martina Braga, OSB, PhD, of Bavaria, Germany. I am also deeply grateful to my friend, speaker and author Stacy Trasancos, PhD, who was generous with her time and scientific input. Her contribution gave me encouragement and confidence. Lastly and most importantly, I must thank the Editor of Word on Fire Votive, Haley Stewart. Working with her has been wonderful, and I am profoundly grateful for her guidance, patience, and organizational skills. To them, and to my supportive family and friends, a heartfelt thanks!
– Ana Braga-Henebry

Special thanks from Word on Fire Votive to Aude Dugast, Dr. Brian Skotko, Shannon Scarfone, Jill Begalle, and Shea Olson.

Votive

WORD ON FIRE

In a world full of noise and distraction, form your imagination with beauty, truth, and goodness!

Word on Fire Votive is a new imprint for children that publishes inspiring stories with stunning illustrations designed to turn young hearts to the Gospel.

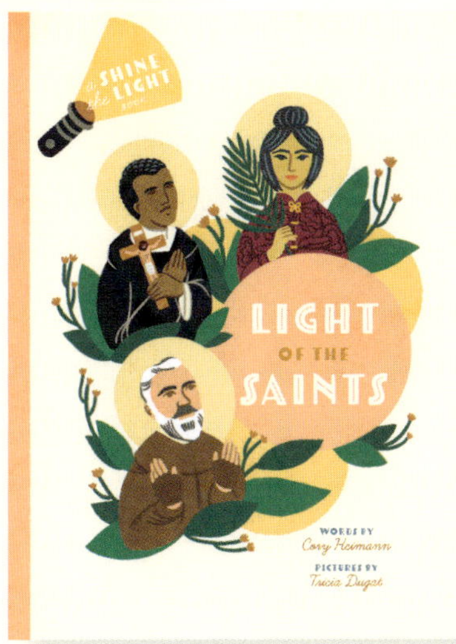

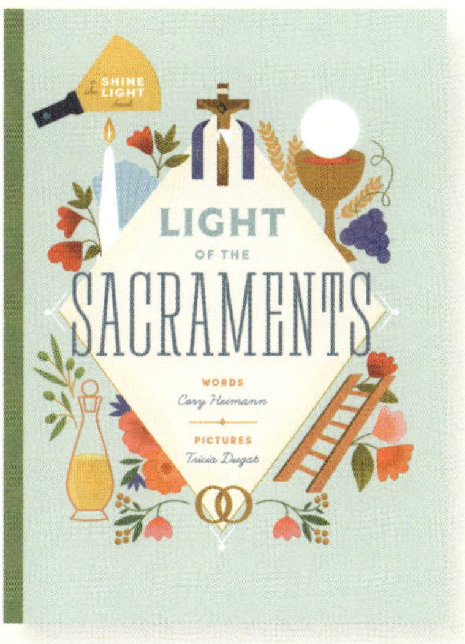

To learn more about our other Votive books, visit

wordonfire.org/votive